PIANO · VOCAL · GUITAR

Music from the Disney Channel Original Movie Soundtrack

© 2017 Disney

ISBN 978-1-4950-9780-5

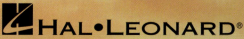

7777 W. BLUEMOUND RD. P.O. BOX 13819 MILWAUKEE, WI 53213

Visit Hal Leonard Online at
www.halleonard.com

WAYS TO BE WICKED

Written By SAM HOLLANDER,
JOSH EDMONDSON, GRANT MICHAELS
and CHARITY DAW

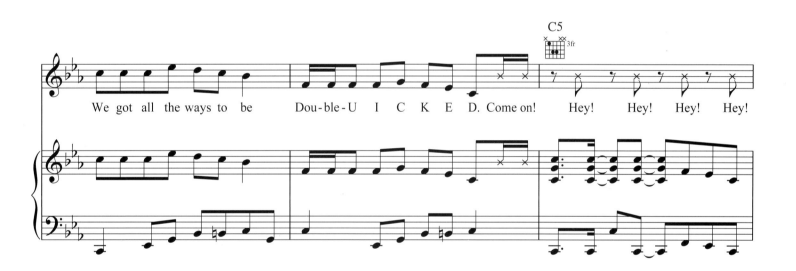

12

WHAT'S MY NAME

Written by ANTONINA ARMATO ,
TIM JAMES, THOMAS STURGES
and ADAM SCHMALHOLZ

Moderate groove

UMA:

This is all hands on deck, call - in' out __ to lost boys and girls. __ I'm gett - in'

tired of the dis - re - spect. We won't stop __ 'til we rule the world. __ It's our time, __ we up next, next. Our

UMA/HARRY:

sail's a - bout __ to be set, set. Ain't seen noth - ing yet. _____ Tell 'em who's in charge so they don't for - get.

* *Recorded a half step lower.*

U-ma, U-ma, la, la, Um.　U-ma, U-ma, la, la, U-ma.　U-ma, U-ma, la, la, Um.　U-ma, U-ma, la, la, Um, U-ma.

UMA:

I'm the queen __ of this town. I call the shots, __ you know who I am, __ I don't need to wear __ no fake crown. Stand

up to me, __ you don't stand a chance. __ It's our time, __ we up next, next. My crew's as real __ as it gets. __ The

UMA/HARRY:

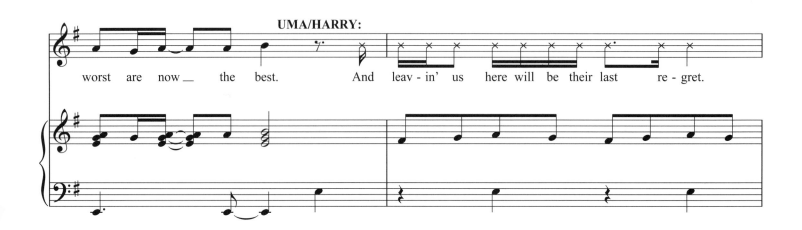

worst are now __ the best. And leav-in' us here will be their last re-gret.

CODA

U - ma, U - ma,

(Lead vocal ad lib. on repeat)

All eyes on me, let me

HARRY/GIL/PIRATES:

U - ma,   U - ma.   U - ma, U - ma, la, la, Um.

see 'em.   What's it, what's it, say it, say it.

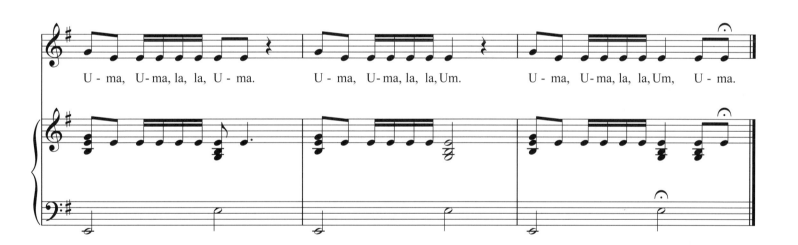

U - ma, U - ma, la, la, U - ma.   U - ma, U - ma, la, la, Um.   U - ma, U - ma, la, la, Um, U - ma.

Additional lyrics

Rap: You know what they say, bad girls have all the fun.
Never learned how to count 'cause I'm number one.
Ready, here we come. We always get our way.
It's a pirate's life every single day.
Hey, she's that captain. I'm the first mate.
Enemy's seasick, can't see straight.
Call 'em fish bait. Throw 'em on a hook.
Uma's so hot they get burned if they look.

CHILLIN' LIKE A VILLAIN

Written by ANTONINA ARMATO,
TIM JAMES, THOMAS STURGES
and ADAM SCHMALHOLZ

Moderate Dance groove

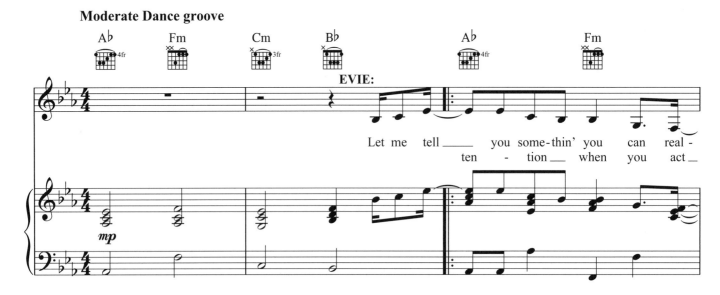

EVIE:

Let me tell ___ you some-thin' you can real-

ten - tion ___ when you act ___

- ly trust, ___ ev-'ry-bod-y's got a wick-ed side. ___ I know you think ___

___ like that. ___ Let us teach ___ you how to dis-ap-pear. ___ You look like you ___

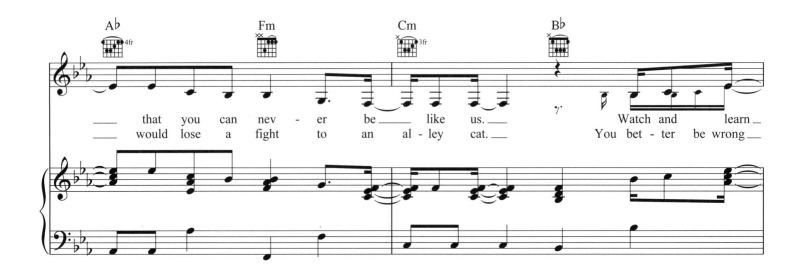

___ that you can nev-er be ___ like us. ___ Watch and learn ___

___ would lose a fight to an al-ley cat. ___ You bet-ter be wrong ___

SPACE BETWEEN

Written by SHAYNA MORDUE,
STEPHEN MARK CONLEY, TYLER SHAMY
and ANDY DODD

IT'S GOIN' DOWN

Written by ANTONINA ARMATO,
TIM JAMES, THOMAS STURGES
and ADAM SCHMALHOLZ

MAL:

I'll throw him overboard and let him swim with killer sharks.   You either hand over the wand or be ripped apart.   Now

let's   all   just   be   smart,   al - though for   you,   that   must   be   hard.   You'll get your wand.   No one

has   to   come   to   an - y   harm.   Don't   try   to   in - tim - i - date. Your   bark   is   much worse than your bite.

Who's   the   bad - dest   of   them   all?   I   guess   we're   find - in'   out   to - night!

PIRATES:

Let's go, bring it on, bet-ter give us what we want. It's the one for the crown. If you don't, it's go-in' down.

VKS:

Let's go, make your move. Peace or war, it's up to you. Give 'em up and do it now.

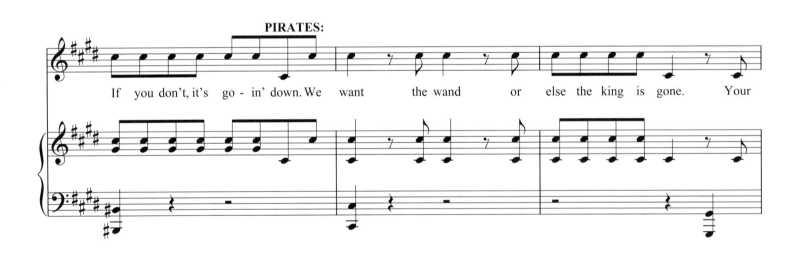

PIRATES:

If you don't, it's go-in' down. We want the wand or else the king is gone. Your

VKS:

time is run-nin' out. You should real-ly watch your mouth. Let's go. Pound for pound,

we're pre-pared to stand our ground. Put your swords up, put 'em up. It's go - in' down.

Yo ___ oh ___ oh. ___ Make the trade. Yo ___ oh ___ oh. ___ Or walk the plank.

C#m/E   C#sus2   C#m/E   C#sus2

N.C.
MAL:

Okay, look. This is not a conversation. It's a do or die situation. If you don't give me back the king, I'll have no hesitation.

I'll serve you right here. And I don't need a reservation.   *That way, your whole pirate crew can have a demonstration.*

Release him now and we can go our separate ways, unless you wanna deal with me.

UMA:

HARRY:

So there's your big speech? An empty ultimatum?   *All it takes is one swing and I'll humiliate him.*

Matter of fact, make one wrong move and I'll debilitate him.   *And if he even starts to swipe, I'll eliminate him.*

D.S. al Coda

For all it takes is one wrong look and I'll... Harry, we get it. Chill.

CODA

A

BEN:

G#

Hey, we don't have to choose. We don't

C#m

have to light the fuse. Mal, __ what-ev-er you do, it's gon-na

B

A

be a lose-lose. There's got-ta be a bet-ter way. __ U-ma, I

PIRATES:

Let's go bring it on. Bring it on, it's go - in' down. Time is run - nin' out.

Bring it on, it's go - in' down. Let's go. Pound for pound we're pre - pared to stand our ground.

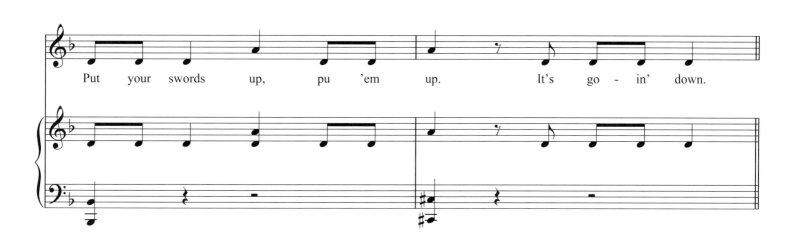

Put your swords up, pu 'em up. It's go - in' down.

YOU AND ME

Written by MITCH ALLAN
and NIKKI LEONTI EDGAR

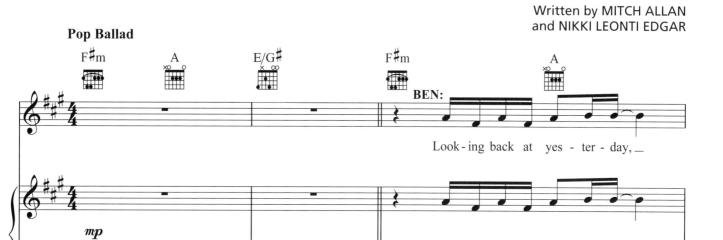

BEN: Look-ing back at yes-ter-day, __

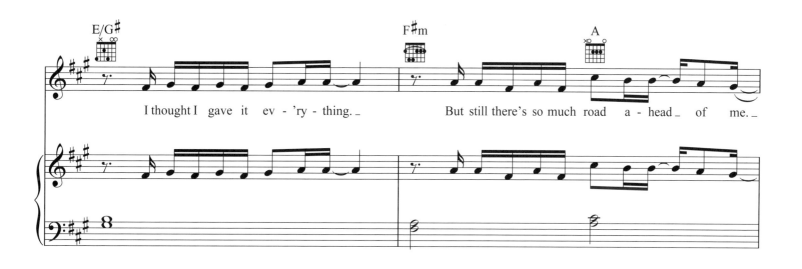

I thought I gave it ev-'ry-thing. __ But still there's so much road a-head __ of me. __

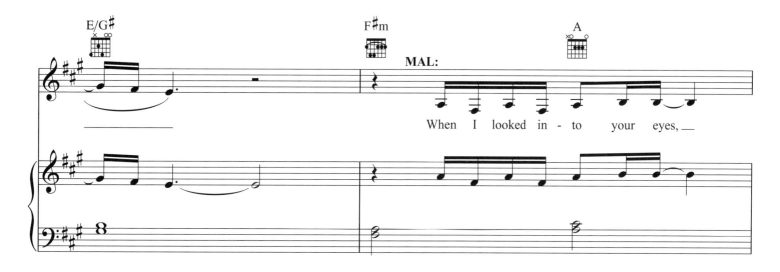

MAL: When I looked in-to your eyes, __

KISS THE GIRL

Music by ALAN MENKEN
Lyrics by HOWARD ASHMAN

With a moderate groove

Oh, oh, — oh, oh. Yeah, yeah, yeah. Come on, come on. Ooh. _____

Oh, oh, — oh, o, oh. Sha la la la la. La la la. Ooh. _____

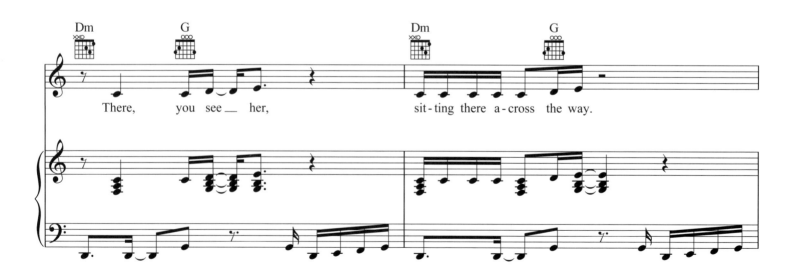

There, you see — her, sit-ting there a-cross the way.

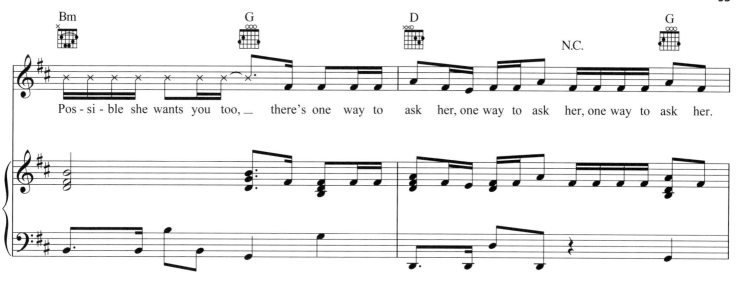

Pos - si - ble she wants you too, __ there's one way to ask her, one way to ask her, one way to ask her.

Oh. _____ No time, _ no time.

Boy, you bet - ter do it soon. No __ time will be bet - ter. It

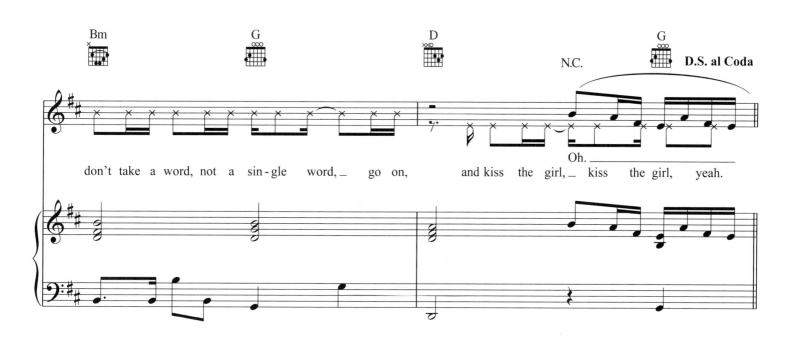

D.S. al Coda

Oh. _____

don't take a word, not a sin - gle word, __ go on, and kiss the girl, __ kiss the girl, yeah.

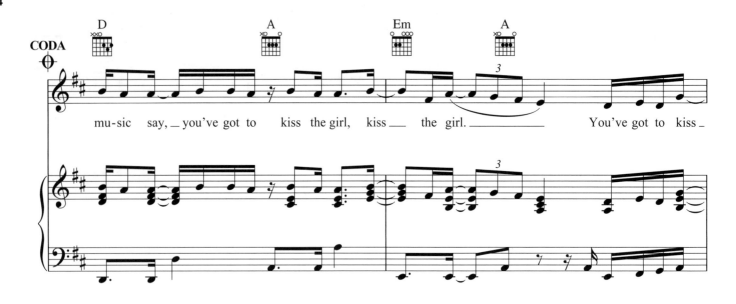

mu-sic say, __ you've got to kiss the girl, kiss __ the girl. _____ You've got to kiss __

__ the girl. _____ You want to kiss __ the girl, _____ you've got to kiss __

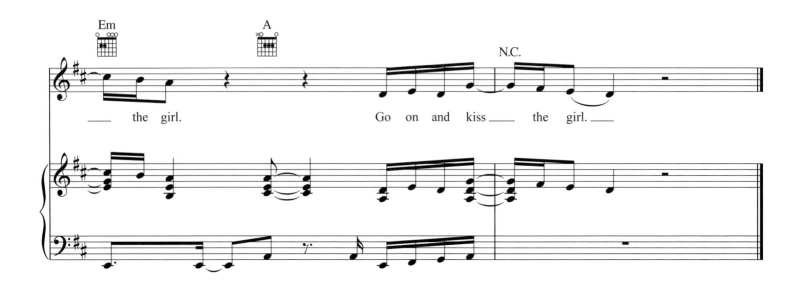

__ the girl. Go on and kiss __ the girl. __

POOR UNFORTUNATE SOULS

Music by ALAN MENKEN
Lyrics by HOWARD ASHMAN

Additional Lyrics

Rap 1: I admit that in the past I've been a nasty.
They weren't kidding when they called me, well, a witch.
But you'll find that nowadays I've mended all my ways,
Repented, seen the light, and made a switch.

And I, fortunately, know a little magic.
It's a talent that I always have possessed.
And here lately–please don't laugh–I use it on behalf
Of the miserable, lonely, and depressed.

Rap 2: Now it's happened once or twice, someone couldn't pay the price,
And I'm afraid I had to rake 'em 'cross the coals.
Yes, I've had the odd complaint, but on the whole
I've been a saint to those poor, unfortunate souls.

Rap 3: The men up there don't like a lot of blabber.
They think a girl who gossips is a bore.
Yes, on land it's much preferred for ladies not to say a word.
And after all, dear, what is idle pratter for?

They're not all that impressed with conversation.
True gentlemen avoid it when they can.
But they dote and swoon and fawn on a lady who's withdrawn,
And she who holds her tongue will get her man.

BETTER TOGETHER

from "Descendants: Wicked World"

Written by JACK KUGELL,
HANNA JONES and MATT WONG

RATHER BE WITH YOU

from "Descendants: Wicked World"

Written by JEANNIE LURIE,
ARIS ARCHONTIS and CHEN NEEMAN

Upbeat Pop

Good, bad, dark knight, what you rath-er be to-night? Would you rath-er
Would you rath-er

eat a bad ap - ple and sleep ___ for a week ___ or break up with your prince? ___
give a big smooch ___ to a frog ___ or dop your phone in - to a bog? ___

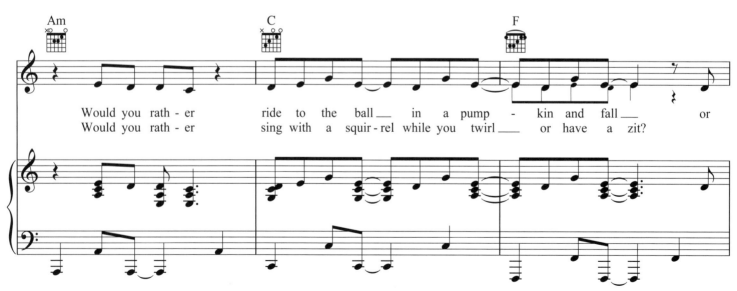

Would you rath - er ride to the ball ___ in a pump - kin and fall ___ or
Would you rath - er sing with a squir - rel while you twirl ___ or have a zit?

EVIL
from "Descendants: Wicked World"

Written by DAN BOOK
and SHELLY PEIKEN

Moderate groove

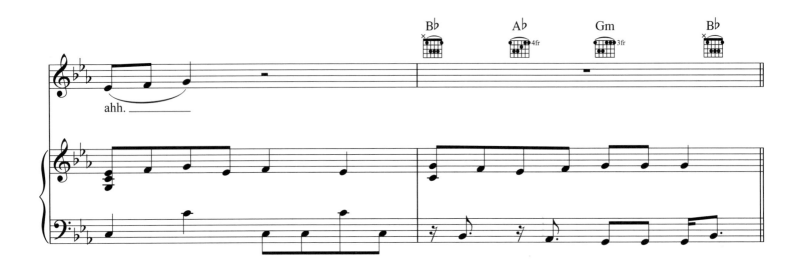